SYNOD OF ASCHHEIM

SYNOD OF ASCHHEIM

TASSILO III DUKE OF BAVARIA

Copyright 2025 by Dalcassian Press

All rights reserved. No part of this book may be reproduced in any manner whatsoever without written permission except in the case of brief quotations embodied in critical articles and reviews.

No part of this publication may be reproduced, distributed, or transmitted in any form or by any means, including photocopying, recording, or other electronic or mechanical methods, without the prior written permission of the publisher, except in the case of brief quotations embodied in critical reviews and certain other non-commercial uses permitted by copyright law. For permission requests, write to Dalcassian Press at admin@thescriptoriumproject.com

Translator: Curtin, D.P. (1985-)

ISBN: 979-8-3492-8703-9 (Paperback)
ISBN: 979-8-3492-8702-2 (eBook)
Library of Congress Control Number:

Printed by Ingram Content Group, 1 Ingram Blvd, La Vergne, Tennessee
First Printing 2025, Dalcassian Press, Wilmington, DE

This work is part of a series produced in association with the Scriptorium Project and its community of scholars and translators.
Please visit our website at: www.thescriptoriumproject.com

INTRODUCTION

The Synod of Aschheim, held in 756 AD in the Bavarian town of Aschheim, marked a significant moment in the religious and political development of early medieval Bavaria and in the German Catholic church. It was convened during a period of increasing Frankish influence in the region and reflected the broader efforts of the Carolingians dynasty to bring the existing ecclesiastical structures in line with Roman Catholic orthodoxy and papal authority. At the heart of the synod was the effort to strengthen the church's moral and doctrinal foundations in the Bavarian duchy, which had been Christianized only a few generations earlier at the tail end of the Merovingian period. Led by St. Boniface, the Anglo-Saxon missionary and papal legate, the synod sought to correct irregularities in church practice and discipline local clergy who were often loosely organized and influenced by remnants of Germanic pagan traditions. Boniface, with papal backing, was determined to unify the Bavarian churches under Roman episcopal leadership, and the Synod of Aschheim became a primary catalyst for implementing these reforms, along with the centralization of Frankish political power in the Carolingian dynasty.

Key outcomes of the synod included the reinforcement of clerical celibacy (then a novel approach to addressing clerical property abuses), the proper consecration of bishops, and the condemnation of simony (the buying and selling of church offices). It also reaffirmed the authority of the See of Rome over the Bavarian church, effectively subordinating local customs to the universal standards of Latin Christianity.

The Synod of Aschheim was not just a religious milestone but also a political one. It showcased the growing alliance between the Carolingian rulers and the Church, particularly through the figure of Duke Tassilo III of Bavaria, a cousin of Charlemagne, who supported the ecclesiastical reforms. This cooperation laid the groundwork for the Carolingian Renaissance and the eventual rise of the institution of the Holy Roman Empire, where church and state worked in unison for general welfare of the German people.

SYNOD OF ASCHHEIM

To our most glorious leader Tassilo, the assembly is directed through these present eulogies in Christ's greeting.

For it is sufficient for Christians to lead their lives according to the norms of the ancient fathers and to ascend to the heights of authority through their teachings, yet due to the diversity of times, it is compelled to address various necessities; therefore, it is holy that the assembly of priests, at appointed times with God's assistance, considers diverse matters according to law. For He who taught our predecessors, the pastors and fathers, will also teach us, as the truth says: As the Father has sent me, so I send you. He sent us who was sent. Therefore, we incessantly give thanks to God, who has established you as a leader in our times, for if in youthful age, you appear more mature in the sense of sacred scripture than your predecessors.

Therefore, fear God and keep His ways; for he who does not have Him placated will never escape His wrath.

I. We command that all, both priests and monks and all clerics by ecclesiastical law, not only in the celebration of masses but also in all liturgical offices, should day and night offer prayers to God for the soul of your wickedness and for the safety of life and kingdom and your faithful ones. And if anyone is found otherwise, let them be deposed.

II. That the churches founded by your ancient predecessors or in your times should remain unharmed without fraud, where the eyes of the Lord contemplate the good and the wicked. Hence, the truth is said through Paul: If anyone destroys the temple of God, etc.

III. On the authority of bishops, who are given the keys of heaven to bind and to loose and exercise pastoral care over the flock, hence they will undoubtedly be accountable, so that they may govern ecclesiastical matters and provide for them wisely. Hence, the Nicene synod says that all ecclesiastical matters should be in the power of the bishops.

IV. Regarding the laws of the churches, with paternal reverence, you should learn and we should be admonished that the whole dispersed world, both east and west, preserves and insinuates the pacts depicted by your predecessors. Whoever attempts to defraud the house of God and its altar by any means, let them be made to swear at the very altar, that you may not alienate from the altar due to their injuries.

V. Concerning the tithes to be rendered to God, the prophet testifies that if anyone does not give the tithe, they should return to the tithe. Hence, it comes about that whoever, either due to the occasion of a priest or out of greed, does not wish to render the tithes to God, let your decree be confirmed, that the church's census be rendered doubly and that your inquiries be culpable according to their possibilities.

VI. Regarding the deacons: that priests should not impose upon themselves except according to the constitution of the bishops, how they may exercise priestly or pastoral care.

VII. That the priests should not attempt to take foreign offerings or tithes for themselves. Hence Gregory says: "He should not send a sickle through a foreign harvest" and elsewhere: "What you do not wish for yourself, do not do to another."

VIII. Concerning abbots and abbesses, it is fitting to admonish that according to their possibilities and the administration of the place, they should live regularly with the provision of the bishops, whose care is known to be present. Hence the truth: Every planting which my Father has not planted, etc.

IX. Concerning clerics and nonnens, that they should either go to the monastery or live regularly with the consent of the bishops, to whom these are entrusted, and if they do not wish to act thus, let them be exterminated.

X. Concerning widows and orphans, it is necessary to admonish them, that they should be made without the calumny of the powerful. Hence the prophet testifies: They will cry out to me, etc.

XI. Concerning the oppression of the poor, it is fitting to admonish that through all presiding judges, centurions, and vicars, you should admonish or command, that they remain without any unjust calumny. Hence the gospel testifies: He has put down the mighty from their thrones and exalted the humble.

XII. Concerning the remaining common people, that they should stand according to the law of the Bavarians, that they may not be alienated from their inheritance, except for capital crimes. Hence the truth: Do not judge, that you may not be judged, etc.; first indeed judgment, afterwards mercy.

XIII. Concerning incestuous marriages, it is fitting that you should follow your decree in all things, which you remember to have constituted in the present public villa of Ascheim. Hence Paul: Nor adulterers will inherit the kingdom of God.

XIV. Regarding your masses throughout the dioceses, that you should deem it worthy to send a certain priest with them, that the innocent may not be deceived by fraud and that money changed due to your fault may return to you, for whom we admit to render an account under the law in due time, or, if you conduct yourself rightly, we believe and testify that you will be rewarded without hesitation on the day of judgment.

XV. Regarding public judgment and the outcry of the poor to be made every Saturday or on the days of the Kalends, that in the ears of your clemency, various acts may be announced. Concerning which days, we dare to testify that you will feast, if you attempt to act thus. And on these days, a priest should always be present, that your judgment may be seasoned with the salt of God, so that earthly judges may not be tormented for the sake of rewards and the innocent may not be oppressed or the guilty justified. — Farewell in Christ.

CONCILIUM ASCHEIMENSE (Latin)

Domino gloriosissimo duce nostro Tassiloni maxime congregatio iura synodali per presentes eulogias in Christo salutem dirigitur.

Sufficit enim Christianis cum normam priscorum patrum vitam deducere et eorum auctoritate passim gradibus polum scandere, tamen propter diversitate temporum diversa necessitate conponendi conpellitur; propterea sanctumque est congregatio sacerdotum indictis temporibus Deo opitulante, ut diversa iure considerentur. Nam qui hos precessores pastores et patres nostros docuit, ipse et nos docebit, sicut veritas ait: Sicut misit me pater, et ego mitto vos. Misit nos qui missus erat. Ideo indesinentes Deo deferimus grates, qui te nostris temporibus constituit principem, quia si in ætate tenerulus, in sensu sanctæ scripturæ precessoribus tuis maturior appareris.

Propterea time Deum et custodi vias eius; nam qui illum non habet placatum numquam evadit iratum.

I. Præcipimus enim, ut omnes tam sacerdotes quam monachi et omnis cleros ecclesiastice iure non tantum in missarum celebritatione, sed etiam in omnibus cursalis oribus tam pro animam scellentiæ vestræ quam pro vitam et regni inlesione et fidelium vestrorum die noctuque preces Deo fundere debeant. Et si aliter quis inventus fuerit, deponatur.

II. Ut ecclesias a priscorum antecessorum vestrorum aut vestris temporibus fundatas sine fraude permanere inlesas debeant, ubi oculi

Domini malos et bonos contemplantur. Unde et veritas per Paulum dicitur: Si quis autem templum Dei violaverit et reliqua.

III. De potestate episcoporum, qui claves polique ligandi atque solvendi deveuntur et curam pastoralem exerceunt in pleve, unde et sine dubio rationem reddituri sunt, ut ecclesiasticis rebus dominentur atque spensando provideant. Unde synodus Nicenensis ait, ut omnes res ecclesiasticas in potestate episcoporum sint.

IV. De legibus ecclesiarum paterna reverentia conperiemini et nos maxime admoneri oportit, quod tot diffusus orbs oriens occidensque conservat et precessorum vestrorum depicta pactus insinuat. Quicumque domum Dei et altarem eius fraudare conatur quibuscumque præsidiis, in ipso altare iurare faciatis, ut ne eorum lesionibus ab altare alienetis.

V. De decimis Deo reddendis profeta testatur, ut, si quis decimam non dederit, ad decimam revertatur. Unde venit, ut quicumque aut occasione presbyteri aut avaritiæ modo Deo decimas reddere noluerit, ut manus vestræ decretus confirmetur, ut dupliciter ecclesiæ censum reddatur et ut vestræ requerillæ secundum possibilitatem culpabilis exsistant.

VI. De deocenis: ut presbyteri sibi minime iniungere debeant nisi secundum constitutionem episcoporum, qualiter sacerdotalem aut pastoralem queant exercere curam.

VII. Ut ipsi presbyteri alienas oblationes aut decimas sibimet minime ingerere conentur. Unde et Gregorius ait: «Per extraneam messem transiens falcem mittere non debet» et alibi: «Quod tibi non vis alii ne facias».

VIII. De abbatibus et abbatissas convenit admonendi, ut secundum possibilitatem et loci administrationem, ut regulariter vivere debeant cum providentia episcoporum, quorum cura hæc adesse dinoscuntur. Unde et veritas: Omnis plantatio, quam non plantavit et reliqua.

IX. De clericis et nonnanes, ut aut in monasterio ire debeant aut cum consensu episcoporum, cui hæc credita sunt, regulariter vivant, et si hoc agere noluerint, exterminentur.

X. De viduis et orfanis admoneri oportit, ut sine calumnias potentium efficientur. Unde profeta testatur: Vociferabuntur ad me et reliqua.

XI. De oppressione pauperorum admonendi convenit, ut per omnia presides seu iudices, centoriones atque vicarios admonere seu præcipere debeatis, ut sine ulla iniusta calumnia permaneant. Unde evangelium testatur: Deposuit potentes de sede et humiles exaltavit.

XII. De reliquo promiscuo vulgo, ut in lege Baiovariorum consistere debeant, ut de eorum hereditate, exceptis capitalis criminibus, non alienentur. Unde veritas: Nolite iudicare, ut non indicabimini et reliqua; primum quidem iudicium, postea misericordia.

XIII. De incestis coniugiis maxime convenit, ut per omnia vestro consequamini decreto, quo in presente villa publica noncupante Aschæim constituere recordamini. Unde et Paulus: Neque adulteri regnum Dei possidebunt.

XIV. De missis vestris per circuitu diocenum, ut ibi quendam sacerdotem cum his mittere dignimini, ut ne innocens fraude deceptus calumnii restuetur et vobis in culpa commutata pecunia recurrat, pro quos in ætate positum sub iure sensu redditurum rationem te reddere fatemus aut, si recte te geris, sine hesitatione remuneraturum in die iudicii esse credimus atque testamur.

XV. De iudicio puplico et clamore pauperorum per singulas sabbatis fiendi aut per dies Kalendarum, ut in auribus clementiæ vestræ acta prænuntient diversa. De quibus diebus te epulaturum fatearis, si hoc agere coneris, testare audemus. Et in his diebus semper sacerdus adesse debeat, ut sit sententia vestra Dei sale condita, ut ne iudices terreni propter præmias causas torquantur et innocentes obprimantur aut nocentes iustificentur. — Valete in Christo.

SYNODE VON ASCHHEIM
(German)

An unseren glorreichen Führer Tassilo, die Versammlung wird durch diese gegenwärtigen Lobpreisungen im Gruß Christi geleitet.

Denn es genügt für die Christen, ihr Leben nach den Normen der alten Väter zu führen und durch ihre Lehren zu den Höhen der Autorität aufzusteigen; doch aufgrund der Vielfalt der Zeiten ist es notwendig, verschiedene Bedürfnisse anzusprechen; daher ist es heilig, dass die Versammlung der Priester zu bestimmten Zeiten mit Gottes Hilfe verschiedene Angelegenheiten gemäß dem Gesetz betrachtet. Denn der, der unseren Vorgängern, den Pastoren und Vätern, gelehrt hat, wird auch uns lehren, wie die Wahrheit sagt: Wie der Vater mich gesandt hat, so sende ich euch. Er hat uns gesandt, der gesandt wurde. Daher danken wir unaufhörlich Gott, der dich in unseren Zeiten als Führer eingesetzt hat, denn wenn du in jugendlichem Alter erscheinst, bist du im Sinne der heiligen Schrift reifer als deine Vorgänger.

Darum fürchte Gott und halte seine Wege; denn wer ihn nicht versöhnt hat, wird niemals seinem Zorn entkommen.

I. Wir befehlen, dass alle, sowohl Priester als auch Mönche und alle Kleriker nach kirchlichem Recht, nicht nur bei der Feier der Messen, sondern auch in allen liturgischen Ämtern, Tag und Nacht Gebete zu Gott für die Seele deiner Bosheit und für die Sicherheit des Lebens und Königreichs und deiner Treuen darbringen. Und wenn jemand anders gefunden wird, lasse man ihn absetzen.

II. Dass die Kirchen, die von deinen alten Vorgängern oder in deinen Zeiten gegründet wurden, unbeschädigt und ohne Betrug bleiben sollen, wo die Augen des Herrn das Gute und das Böse betrachten. Daher wird die Wahrheit durch Paulus gesagt: Wenn jemand den Tempel Gottes zerstört, usw.

III. Auf die Autorität der Bischöfe, die die Schlüssel des Himmels erhalten haben, um zu binden und zu lösen und das pastorale Amt über die Herde auszuüben, werden sie daher zweifellos verantwortlich sein, damit sie kirchliche Angelegenheiten weise regeln und für sie sorgen können. Daher sagt das Konzil von Nicäa, dass alle kirchlichen Angelegenheiten in der Macht der Bischöfe sein sollten.

IV. Hinsichtlich der Gesetze der Kirchen, mit väterlicher Ehrfurcht, solltest du lernen und wir sollten ermahnt werden, dass die ganze verstreute Welt, sowohl Osten als auch Westen, die von deinen Vorgängern geschaffenen Pakte bewahrt und insinuieren sollte. Wer auch immer versucht, das Haus Gottes und seinen Altar auf irgendeine Weise zu betrügen, lasse ihn am Altar schwören, damit du nicht aufgrund ihrer Verletzungen vom Altar entfremdet wirst.

V. Über die Zehnten, die Gott zu geben sind, bezeugt der Prophet, dass, wenn jemand den Zehnten nicht gibt, er zum Zehnten zurückkehren sollte. Daher kommt es, dass wer auch immer, sei es aufgrund der Gelegenheit eines Priesters oder aus Gier, nicht bereit ist, die Zehnten Gott zu geben, dein Dekret bestätigt werden soll, dass die Kirchensteuer doppelt erhoben wird und dass deine Nachforschungen nach ihren Möglichkeiten schuldhaft sind.

VI. Über die Diakone: dass Priester sich nicht selbst auferlegen sollten, außer gemäß der Verfassung der Bischöfe, wie sie das priesterliche oder pastorale Amt ausüben können.

VII. Dass die Priester nicht versuchen sollten, fremde Gaben oder Zehnten für sich selbst zu nehmen. Daher sagt Gregor: "Er sollte keine Sichel durch eine fremde Ernte senden" und anderswo: "Was du dir nicht wünschst, tue nicht einem anderen."

VIII. Über Äbte und Äbtissinnen ist es passend, zu ermahnen, dass sie gemäß ihren Möglichkeiten und der Verwaltung des Ortes regelmäßig mit der Versorgung der Bischöfe leben sollten, deren Fürsorge bekanntlich gegenwärtig ist. Daher die Wahrheit: Jedes Pflanzen, das mein Vater nicht gepflanzt hat, usw.

IX. Über Kleriker und Nonnen, dass sie entweder ins Kloster gehen oder regelmäßig mit dem Einverständnis der Bischöfe leben sollten, denen diese anvertraut sind, und wenn sie nicht so handeln wollen, lasse sie ausgerottet werden.

X. Über Witwen und Waisen ist es notwendig, sie zu ermahnen, dass sie ohne die Verleumdung der Mächtigen gemacht werden sollten. Daher bezeugt der Prophet: Sie werden zu mir schreien, usw.

XI. Über die Unterdrückung der Armen ist es passend zu ermahnen, dass durch alle vorsitzenden Richter, Zenturionen und Vikare du ermahnen oder befehlen solltest, dass sie ohne ungerechte Verleumdung bleiben. Daher bezeugt das Evangelium: Er hat die Mächtigen von ihren Thronen gestürzt und die Demütigen erhoben.

XII. Über die übrigen einfachen Leute, dass sie gemäß dem Gesetz der Bayern stehen sollten, damit sie nicht von ihrem Erbe entfremdet werden, außer bei Kapitalverbrechen. Daher die Wahrheit: Urteilt nicht, damit ihr nicht gerichtet werdet, usw.; zuerst tatsächlich das Urteil, danach die Barmherzigkeit.

XIII. Über inzestuöse Ehen ist es passend, dass du deinem Dekret in allen Dingen folgst, das du erinnerst, in der gegenwärtigen öffentlichen Villa von Ascheim festgelegt zu haben. Daher Paulus: Noch Ehebrecher werden das Reich Gottes erben.

XIV. Über deine Messen in den Diözesen, dass du es für würdig erachten solltest, einen bestimmten Priester mit ihnen zu senden, damit die Unschuldigen nicht durch Betrug getäuscht werden und das Geld, das aufgrund deines Fehlers gewechselt wurde, zu dir zurückkehrt, für den wir zu gegebener Zeit unter dem Gesetz Rechenschaft ablegen, oder, wenn du dich recht verhältst, glauben und bezeugen wir, dass du am Tag des Gerichts ohne Zögern belohnt wirst.

XV. Über das öffentliche Urteil und das Geschrei der Armen, das jeden Samstag oder an den Tagen der Kalenden erhoben werden soll, dass in den Ohren deiner Milde verschiedene Taten angekündigt werden können. Über welche Tage wir es wagen zu bezeugen, dass du festlich feiern wirst, wenn du versuchst, so zu handeln.

Und an diesen Tagen sollte immer ein Priester anwesend sein, damit euer Urteil mit dem Salz Gottes gewürzt wird, damit irdische Richter nicht um der Belohnungen willen gequält werden und die Unschuldigen nicht unterdrückt oder die Schuldigen gerechtfertigt werden. — Lebt wohl in Christus.

This work was produced in association with:

www.ingramcontent.com/pod-product-compliance
Lightning Source LLC
LaVergne TN
LVHW061623070526
838199LV00078B/7405